jB OR
Kirkpatrick, Rob.
Jeff Gordon

Jasper County Public Library System

Overdue notices are a courtesy of
the library system.
Failure to receive an overdue notice
does not absolve the borrower of the
obligation to return materials on time.

READING POWER

Jeff Gordon
NASCAR Champion

Rob Kirkpatrick

The Rosen Publishing Group's
PowerKids Press ™
New York

1

For JD and his family.

Published in 2000 by The Rosen Publishing Group, Inc.
29 East 21st Street, New York, NY 10010

First Edition

Book design: Maria Melendez

Photo Credits: pp. 5, 7, 11, 13, 17, 21 © David Taylor/Allsport; pp. 9, 15, 22 © Craig Jones/Allsport; p. 19 © Jamie Squire/Allsport.

Text Consultant: Linda J. Kirkpatrick, Reading Specialist/Reading Recovery Teacher

Kirkpatrick, Rob.
     Jeff Gordon : NASCAR champion / by Rob Kirkpatrick.
     p. cm. — (Reading power)
  Includes index.
     SUMMARY: Introduces Jeff Gordon, the NASCAR driver who won the Daytona 500 in 1999.
     ISBN 0-8239-5544-3 (lib. bdg.)
     1. Gordon, Jeff, 1971– Juvenile literature. 2. Automobile racing drivers—United States Biography Juvenile literature. [1. Gordon, Jeff, 1971– 2. Automobile racing drivers.] I. Title. II. Series.
     GV1032.G67 K57 1999
     796.72'092—dc21
     [B]   99-32385
                                     CIP

Manufactured in the United States of America

Contents

Jeff Gordon races cars. He is a NASCAR driver.

Jeff needs a helmet when he is racing.

Jeff goes very fast in his car.

Jeff races on a track. Lots of cars race around the track.

11

Jeff's car is number 24.
He drives a Chevrolet.

13

Lots of people come to NASCAR races. They like to see Jeff race.

Jeff gets a lot of money when he wins a race.

WINSTON NO BULL 5

ston Cup Series

O THE
R OF

Jeff Gordon
One Million & 00⁄00

BRICKYARD 400

MO

In 1999, Jeff won a big race. It was the Daytona 500. This race is in Florida.

When Jeff needs help, he makes a pit stop. His team helps fix his car.

21

Jeff's wife, Brooke, likes to see his races. She is very happy when he wins.

Here is a good book to read about Jeff Gordon:

Jeff Gordon (NASCAR Track Sounds)
Futech Interactive Products

To learn more about NASCAR, check out these Web sites:

http://sikids.com/shorter/gordon/index/html
http://sikids.com/racing/overdrive/index.html

Glossary

Chevrolet (shev-roh-LAY) The name of a type of car.

helmet (HEL-mit) What a driver wears to keep his head safe.

NASCAR (NAZ-kahr) National Association for Stock Car Auto Racing.

pit stop (PIT STOP) When a driver goes off the track to get his car fixed.

track (TRAK) A round place where people race cars.

Index

Word Count: 116

Note to Librarians, Teachers, and Parents

If reading is a challenge, Reading Power is a solution! Reading Power is perfect for readers who want high-interest subject matter at an accessible reading level. These fact-filled, photo-illustrated books are designed for readers who want straightforward vocabulary, engaging topics, and a manageable reading experience. With clear picture/text correspondence, leveled Reading Power books put the reader in charge. Now readers have the power to get the information they want and the skills they need in a user-friendly format.